Spirit Flows

POWERFUL SCRIPTURES,
BEAUTIFUL PICTURES
and a
REFLECTIVE MIXTURE

Dr. Marjorie E. Miles

Spirit Flows

©2021 Dr. Marjorie E. Miles

Print ISBN 978-1-09838-442-5 | eBook ISBN 978-1-09838-443-2

Especially For

_____

From

_____

Date

_____

Dedicated

to the

Uplifting

of

God's Kingdom

and the

Evolution

of the

Soul

TABLE OF CONTENTS

I. John 1:1 1

II. Isaiah 55:11 4

III. Matthew 24:35 9

IV. Proverbs 18:21 13

V. Hebrews 11:1, 3 16

VI. Hebrews 11:6 21

VII. Matthew 7:7-8 25

VIII. Matthew 6:33 29

IX. Matthew 21:22 32

X. James 4:2 33

XI. Romans 12:2-3 36

XII. Hebrews 8:10 41

XIII. Proverbs 3:5-6 44

XIV. Luke 17:20-21 49

XV. 1 Corinthians 2:14-16 52

XVI. Psalm 23 56

XVII. James 1:6-8 (KJV) 62

XVIII. Psalm 46:10 66

XIX. Ecclesiastes 3: 1-8 71

XX. II Corinthians 5: 1-8 75

XXI. I Corinthians 15: 50-55 79

XXII. Psalm 24:1-3 83

XXIII. Luke 12:27-29 86

XXIV. I Chronicles 4:10 95

XXV. II Corinthians 4:18 99

XXVI. Galatians 5:22-25 103

XXVII. Matthew 6:8-12 107

XXVIII. John 3:5-8 111

XXIX. Mark 4: 35-41 114

ACKNOWLEDGMENTS

This spiritual guide would not have been possible without the contributions of so many people. My sincere thanks and lots of love to all who supported and contributed to this book.

Brandon Bennett
Granville Cannon
Bianca Cropper
Briana Cropper
Fran Cropper
Kara Harris
Justin Miles
Tyrone Miles
Lusana Reid
Andrew Waters
Edwin Waters

Note: Scriptures from the King James Version of the Bible were used in this book. There are three (3) photos in this book that were take from the internet sources. One photo is free and two were purchased. One picture was purchased from GoGraph (p.4). The second picture was purchased IStock (p.104) with all rights and privileges (please see their website for licensing and use agreements).

INTRODUCTION

As you read the powerful scriptures in this book, it is my prayer that you will read each scripture with spiritual eyes rather than your carnal eyes. When you look at each picture, I pray that you see God in all of His glorious creations. Lastly, take the time to reflect on the meaning of the scripture in your life. Where do you see Him? Do you see Him in yourself, the birds, the bees, and in the flowers? See if you can feel Him in the very air that you breathe? God does not make mistakes, so it is no mistake that you are reading this book. Reading and reflecting will allow you to spend time with the Master.

You are invited to use the scriptures in this book to write the word of God on your heart. Writing God's words on your heart means that you can access the power of the living word of God when you find yourself in times of trouble. His words will comfort you, heal you and provide you with the wisdom that you need to get through any situation. You are invited to ease into the natural, effortless, unfolding and transformative power of the flow of Spirit, as described by Belitz and Lundstrom (1998) in their book *The Power of Flow: Practical Ways to Transform Your Life with Meaningful Coincidence.*

Each of the powerful scriptures in this book is followed by a nugget of faith and an opportunity to reflect. Journaling helps you with witnessing and reflecting upon your life. What trials and tribulations have you overcome? Journaling, reflecting, and witnessing allows you to look back over your life, over the time that has passed, and evaluate the good, the bad, and the ugly. It also holds up a mirror to your soul that reflects to you those things that still need to be worked on. Remember, "all things work together for good to those who love God, to those who are the called according to His purpose (Romans 8:28). Read the scriptures, meditate on His word, and you will discover who you are and your purpose in life, which is to serve Him.

JOHN 10:27-30

My sheep hear My voice, and I know them, and they follow Me. And I give them eternal life, and they shall never perish; neither shall anyone snatch them out of My hand. My Father who has given them to Me, is greater than all; and no one is able to snatch them out of My Father's hand. I and My Father are one.

JOHN 1:1

In the beginning was the Word, and the Word was
with God, and the Word was God.

DEUTERONOMY 11:18

Therefore, you shall lay up these words of mine in
your heart and in your soul, and bind them as
a sign on your hand, and they shall be as frontlets
between your eyes.

A NUGGET OF FAITH

You may ask: How do I lay God's Word on my heart? Commit to
make time for God's Word by:

- Reading God's Word,

- Speaking God's Word,

- Listening to God's Word,

- Praying God's Word,

- Singing God's Word,

- Sharing God's Word,

- Memorizing God's Word.

Can you add to this list? In order to commit, you must use the Word
of God to build your Faith!

DATE

Reflections

DATE

Isaiah 55:11

So shall My word be that goes forth from My
mouth; it shall not return to Me void, but it shall
accomplish what I please and it shall prosper in the
thing for which I sent it.

A Nugget of Faith

Everything starts with the spoken Word! Speak over yourself and
encourage yourself to use God's Word because the Word will not
return to you void. So why not speak peace, love, joy, prosperity, life,
kindness, and health. Speak life to your children, your spouse, your
sister, your brother, your aunts and your uncles. Then step back and
see what God can do. It is much easier to speak positive fruits of the
spirit than it is to speak negative thoughts all day long. The negative
thoughts will make you tired and worry. Try changing the words you
speak, and you will change your life!

Reflections

_____

_____

_____

_____

_____

_____

_____

_____

_____

_____

_____

_____

_____

_____

_____

Reflections

DATE

MATTHEW 24:35

Heaven and earth will pass away,
but My words will by no means pass away.

A NUGGET OF FAITH

Words have meaning! And, as we can see from Genesis and in our own lives, words have creative power. The living Word of God is the same yesterday, today, and tomorrow. The Word is so powerful that there are no mortal words that can describe the Great I AM. The sooner you can experience that God is, the sooner you can experience, God for yourself. This is an experience that only you can have with GOD, no one else can do it for you! So, stay committed and seek him for yourself! Look at the picture. Meditate on the picture. Can you see Him? Can you feel Him?

Reflections

_____
DATE

....

....

....

....

....

....

....

....

....

....

....

....

....

....

Reflections

_____

DATE

....

....

....

....

....

....

....

....

....

....

....

....

....

....

Proverbs 18:21

Death and life are in the power of the tongue, and
those who love it will eat its fruit.

A Nugget of Faith

There is life and death in the power of the tongue. Words can lift you up or tear you down. Words can heal you or kill you. Kind words are like a honeycomb, sweetness to the soul and health to the bones (Proverbs 16:24), while harsh words can sting like vinegar or salt in a freshly opened wound. You can hang your entire life on the words of the story that comes out of your mouth. Change your words, change your mind, and it will change your life. Do not allow yourself to be hung by the tongue. Speak life!

A wise woman once said, "God gave us two ears and one mouth, so we can listen more than we talk: therefore, when you are talking, be mindful of your words."

Reflections

DATE

Reflections

_____

DATE

....

....

....

....

....

....

....

....

....

....

....

....

....

....

Hebrews 11:1, 3

(1) Now Faith is the substance of things hoped for,
the evidence of things not seen.
(3) By faith we understand that the worlds were
framed by the word of God, so that the things
which are seen were not made of things which
are visible.

A Nugget of Faith

It is through scripture that we see the creative power of the Word, which is God. The Word joins with faith in manifold wisdom to make those things that are not seen, come into physical reality so they can be seen. Be very careful about what you pray for, as your words have manifesting power. It is the energy power of words by which the world and everything in it was created! Furthermore, you must believe that you will receive what you speak out of your mouth. However, James 2:17 warns us that faith by itself, if it does not have works, is dead.

Faith Without Works Is Dead!

Reflections

_____

DATE

....

....

....

....

....

....

....

....

....

....

....

....

....

....

....

....

....

....

....

....

Reflections

DATE

....

....

....

....

....

....

....

....

....

....

....

....

....

....

BELIEVE, HAVE FAITH, AND RECEIVE

HEBREWS 11:6

But without faith it is impossible to please Him,
for he who comes to God must believe that He is,
and that He is a rewarder of those who diligently
seek Him.

A NUGGET OF FAITH

George Washington Carver said, Believe. The promises of God are real. They are as real, as solid, yes infinitely more solid than this table, which the materialistic so thoroughly believe in. If you would only believe, O ye of little faith. Do not wait for something to go wrong to test your faith. Begin today to feed your faith now and you will be deeply rewarded when times of trouble come to test your faith. There is an old cliché that says feed your faith, starve your fears to death. Where is your faith? How does your faith hold up in troubled times and when you are afraid?

Reflections

_____

DATE

Reflections

DATE

MATTHEW 7:7-8

Ask, and it will be given to you;

seek, and you will find;

knock, and it will be opened to you.

For everyone who asks receives,

and he who seeks finds,

and to him who knocks it will be opened.

A NUGGET OF FAITH

The concept of knocking is about you actively seeking Him and asking Him to open the door for your salvation, which only He can do. Your salvation is a gift from God. Doesn't that make Him worth you standing at the door, knocking, and seeking to experience God for yourself? There are times when the door does not open readily. It is important to understand that delay does not mean denial. Sometimes, however, when we see what is on the other side of the door, we will thank God for that closed door and trust in Him.

Reflections

_____

DATE

Reflections

DATE

MATTHEW 6:33

But seek first the kingdom of God and His
Righteousness, and all these things shall be added
unto you.

A NUGGET OF FAITH

The asking is in the power of the spoken Word. Many times, we get
not because we ask not. The seeking is in your commitment to keep
looking for the spirit of God that lives in you, me and in all things!
The real question is: Do you have the courage and the commitment
to keep seeking?

Reflections

_____

DATE

Reflections

DATE

MATTHEW 21:22

"And whatever things you ask in prayer, believing,
you will receive."

**Be careful what you pray for, because you
just might get it; and when you get it, you
might not want it!**

A NUGGET OF FAITH

Many times, we get not, because we ask not (James 4:2). Too often
we are so busy asking for those worldly things that we forget to ask
for Godly things. We forget to ask God or the Holy Spirit to come
into our lives. We forget to ask for love, peace, joy, kindness, and
gentleness. Remember, we serve a jealous God. He tells us that we
should have no other God before him. Today we find people spending more time with social media and the television before seeking
out and spending time with God. Think about how much time you
actually spend seeking God and asking Him for Godly things. My
mother used to say be careful what you pray for, because you just
might get it; and, when you get it you might want to give it back. Ask
for Godly things, which will bring you peace, love, joy, prosperity,
health, and the ability to serve your fellow man and woman.

JAMES 4:2

Yet, you do not have because you do not ask.

Reflections

DATE

Reflections

DATE

....

....

....

....

....

....

....

....

....

....

....

....

....

....

....

Romans 12:2-3

And do not be conformed to this world, but be
transformed by the renewing of your mind, that you
may prove what is good and acceptable and perfect
will of God.
For I say, through the grace given to me, to everyone
who is among you, not to think of himself more
highly than he ought to think, but to think soberly,
as God has dealt to each one a measure of faith.

Be Transformed by the Renewing of
Your Mind

A Nugget of Faith

In order to renew you mind you must put aside those things that are
of this world and renew your mind with God's Word. Use the measure of faith that God has given to you. Commit to faith, commit
to seeking Him, and align yourself with His Word. Your old mental
programming will no longer serve you in today's world. What steps
are you going to take to renew your mind?

Reflections

DATE

....

....

....

....

....

....

....

....

....

....

....

....

....

....

....

....

....

....

Reflections

DATE

HEBREWS 8:10

For this is the covenant that I will make with the
house of Israel after those days, says the Lord. I put
My law in their mind and write it on their hearts;
and I will be their God and they shall be My People.

A NUGGET OF FAITH

One might ask, how does the Word of God get written on the heart?
It is reiterated that you must read the Word, speak the Word, listen to
the Word, meditate on the Word and ultimately the Word becomes
flesh. When the law is steadfastly written in your heart, your Spirit
will quicken. When your Spirit quickens your conscience bears wit-
ness to your thoughts either accusing or defending them. The God of
your own understanding will be aligned with the Christ consciousness that comes about when you renew your mind. Given the times
that we live in, isn't it time to write His words on your heart and in
your mind. II Chronicles 7:14 summarizes the importance of having his word written on our hearts and minds because it aligns with
the times in which we are now living. II **Chronicles 7:14** states, If
My people who are called by My name will humble themselves, and
pray and seek My face, and turn from their wicked ways, then I will
hear from heaven, and will forgive their sins and heal their land.

PSALMS 119:11

Your word I have hidden in my heart, that I might
not sin against You.

DATE

Reflections

_____

DATE

Proverbs 3:5-6

Trust in the Lord with all your heart, and lean
not on your own understanding; In all your ways
acknowledge Him and He shall direct your paths.

A Nugget of Faith

For many years, my prayer partner was my sister-in-law. She recited this scripture so many times, that I committed it to memory. At that time, I believe her trials and tribulations were many. When I started having some very tough trials and tribulations of my own; I used it all the time to knock down the devil and destroy the chaos that he was attempting to create in my life. As I learned more about spiritual warfare, I begin to know how necessary it was to have God's Word committed to memory, because I did not know what I would need or when I would need it.

Reflections

_____

DATE

....

....

....

....

....

....

....

....

....

....

....

....

....

....

....

....

Reflections

DATE

....

....

....

....

....

....

....

....

....

....

....

....

....

....

....

Luke 17:20-21

Now when He was asked by the Pharisees when the kingdom of God would come. He answered them and said, "The kingdom of God does not come with observation; Nor will they say, 'See here!' or 'See there!'

For indeed the kingdom of God is within you."

A Nugget of Faith

You will not be able to understand any of God's Word with a carnal mind. You must approach God through spirit, truth and love. You must approach Him with wide-eyed wonder, and as though you are a child, and He is your Father. In fact, He has sent a helper by way of the Holy Spirit to give you a spirit of discernment as to who you are and your purpose in this world. Follow the flow of the Holy Spirit and let Him in!

Reflections

DATE

....

....

....

....

....

....

....

....

....

....

....

....

....

....

....

....

....

....

....

....

....

....

Reflections

_____

DATE

1 Corinthians 2:14-16

But the natural man does not receive the things of
the Spirit of God, for they are foolishness to him;
nor can he know them, because they are spiritu-
ally discerned.
But he who is spiritual judges all things, yet he himself is rightly judged by no one.
For "who has known the mind of the Lord that he
may instruct Him?" But we have the mind of Christ.

A Nugget of Faith

What does it mean to have the mind of Christ? Christ Consciousness requires you to spend time seeking the Great I Am. The foolishness, or suffering that people go through is not necessary and can be overcome with a Christ Consciousness. The mind of Christ allows you to rise above all of earth's foolishness and sorrow. There is a hymn with a line in it that says, "Earth has no sorrow that heaven cannot heal." Having a Christ mindset, forces you to ask the question, "What would Jesus do?"

Reflections

DATE

....

....

....

....

....

....

....

....

....

....

....

....

....

....

....

....

....

....

....

....

....

....

Reflections

DATE

....

....

....

....

....

....

....

....

....

....

....

....

....

....

....

....

....

....

....

....

....

....

....

....

PSALM 23

The Lord is my Shepherd; I shall not want.

He makes me to lie down in green pastures; He
leads me beside the still waters.
He restores my soul; He leads me in the paths of
righteousness for His name's sake.

Yea, though I walk through the valley of the shadow
of death, I shall fear no evil; for You are with me;
Your rod and Your staff, they comfort me.

You prepare a table before me in the presence of
my enemies; You anoint my head with oil; my cup
runs over.

Surely goodness and mercy shall follow me all the
days of my life; and I will dwell in the house of the
LORD forever.

A Nugget of Faith

This Psalm is an old-time favorite worth committing to memory. It is short and sweet. Memorizing this Psalm writes the Word in your heart so you can speak it out of your mouth when you have a need. There will be times when you will need to feel comforted by God and commune with Him in spirit and in truth. Regardless of the kind of trials or tribulations, this Psalm is always a source of strength and inspiration.

Reflections

DATE

....

....

....

....

....

....

....

....

....

....

....

....

....

....

....

....

Reflections

DATE

James 1:6-8 (KJV)

But let him **ask in faith, with no doubting,** for he who doubts is like a wave of the sea driven and tossed by the wind. For let not the man suppose that he will receive anything from the Lord: He is a double-minded man, unstable in all of his ways.

A Nugget of Faith

A double-minded man is a person who is restless and confused in his thoughts. The mind rumbles and tumbles like the wind. In Eastern religions the mind that rumbles and tumbles is called the "monkey mind." Fear not! There is a way to calm the monkey mind. The solution is to: (1) be still, (2) meditate on His Word, and (3) commit to a consistent practice.

If you are confused about whether you can tear down mountains, barriers, or strong holds, then you are double-minded. The mountain that does not move is about the uncertainty in your mind. The mountain that does not move is not about God's promise to move those obstacles out of the way. Remember that you are a co-creator with God and that God cannot lie. You must ask yourself how you can strengthen your mindset. How will you commit to a practice of stillness, meditating on the Word of God so that you tame the monkey mind and harness the power of God that lives within you?

Reflections

_____

DATE

....

....

....

....

....

....

....

....

....

....

....

....

....

....

Reflections

_____

DATE

....

....

....

....

....

....

....

....

....

....

....

....

....

....

....

....

....

....

....

....

....

....

PSALM 46:10

Be still, and know that I am God

A NUGGET OF FAITH

There comes a time in your life when you must "Be Still" and know that God is God all by himself or herself! Where is your sanctuary or your quiet place to pray: a closet, a walk, sitting in nature, or a garden, perhaps? Find your place to be still and pray. This will also give God time to speak to you. We often use all of our time with God asking for this or that, and we never give him his time to truly speak to our hearts! Too often, we spend time with friends or in front of some device and not enough time with God. As of this moment, rethink your quiet time with God. Think about when, and where your sanctuary will be. Take time now to reflect on how you will spend more of your time with God. Practice listening, as it is a skill that many of us need to work on developing. Being quiet and still, creates inner space that is necessary to hear God speak to you. The key is to make this your daily practice.

Reflections

DATE

....
....
....
....
....
....
....
....
....
....
....
....
....
....
....
....
....
....
....
....
....
....

Reflections

DATE

....

....

....

....

....

....

....

....

....

....

....

....

....

....

....

....

EXAMINE THE SEASONS OF YOUR LIFE

ECCLESIASTES 3: 1-8

To everything there is a season, a time for every purpose under heaven: A time to be born, and a time
to die; a time to plant, and a time to pluck what is
planted; A time to kill, and a time to heal; a time to
break down, and a time to build up; A time to weep,
and a time to laugh, a time to mourn, and a time
to dance; A time to cast away stones, and a time
to gather stones; a time to embrace, and a time to
refrain from embracing; A time to gain, and a time
to lose; a time to keep, time to throw away; A time
to tear, and a time to sew; a time to keep silence,
and a time to speak; A time to love, and a time to
hate; a time of war, and a time of peace.

A NUGGET OF FAITH

What time is it for you? What season of life are you in? What cycles
have you gone through? How are you changing in each season
of your life? In whatever season you are in, or whatever the time,
remember that it is always God time! God is always there for you!
When you transition from this life into the next God will ask you,
"How did you use the time that I gave you?"

Reflections

DATE

Reflections

....

....

....

....

....

....

....

....

....

....

....

....

....

....

....

II Corinthians 5: 1-8

For we know that if our earthly house, *this* tent*, is destroyed, we have a building from God, a house not made with hands, eternal in the heavens.

For in this we groan, earnestly desiring to be clothed with our habitation which is from heaven.

If indeed, having been clothed, we shall not be found naked.

For we who are in *this* tent groan, being burdened, burdened, not because we want to be unclothed, but further clothed, that mortality may be swallowed up by life.

Now He who has prepared us for this very thing is God, who also has given us the Spirit as a guarantee.

So we are always confident, knowing that while we are at home in the body, we are absent from the Lord.

For we walk by faith, not by sight,

We are confident, yes, well pleased rather to be absent from the body and to be present with the Lord.

tent refers to the body

A Nugget of Faith

"Fear Not" or "Be not afraid" can be found in the King James Version of the Bible 103 times (soulshepherding.org). Corinthians I and II provides you with an opportunity to come face-to-face with your mortality and your immortality. Meditating on the words of these two books of the Bible allow you to know that when you embrace your Spiritual self you have victory over death! Read the living Word and grasp your immortality. Reach out and touch that spiritual being that lives in that physical tent known as the body. It is a gift from the living God and there is nothing you can do to earn it. Be still and embrace your spirit!

Reflections

DATE

Reflections

DATE

....

....

....

....

....

....

....

....

....

....

....

....

....

....

....

I Corinthians 15: 50-55

Now this I say, brethren, that flesh and blood cannot

inherit the kingdom of God; nor does corruption

inherit incorruption.

Behold, I tell you a mystery: We shall not all sleep,

but we shall all be changed -

In a moment, in the twinkling of an eye, at the

last trumpet. For the trumpet will sound, and the

dead will be raised incorruptible, and we shall

be changed.

For this corruptible must put on incorruption, and

this mortal must put on immortality. So when this

corruptible has put on incorruption, and this mortal

has put on immortality, then shall be brought to pass

the saying that is written: "Death is swallowed up

in victory."

"O, Death where is your sting? O Hades, where is

your victory?"

A Nugget of Faith

Unleash your faith! Meditate on the words of the scripture, I Corinthians 15: 50-56. Find your quiet space where you can tune into your spiritual self. You cannot find yourself in the midst of the world's chaos and expect to find peace, nor salvation. Come face-to-face with your mortality. In the spiritual world death has no victory. Acknowledge your power as a spiritual being having a physical experience!

Reflections

DATE

Reflections

DATE

PSALM 24:1-3

The earth is the Lord's and all its fullness, the world
and those who dwell therein. For He has founded
it upon the seas, and established it upon the waters.
Who may ascend into the hill of the Lord? Or who
may stand in His holy place?

A NUGGET OF FAITH

When I read this Psalm, I am reminded of the words of Thomas
quoted in the book Beyond Belief: The Secret Gospel of Thomas
(Pagel, 2003). Jesus was asked "When will the kingdom come?'
Thomas's Jesus says "It will not come by waiting for it. It will not be
a matter of saying, 'Here it is,' or 'There it is.' Rather, the kingdom
of the Father (which I believe to be heaven) is spread upon the earth
and people do not see it." Again, the kingdom of God is within and
cannot be seen with carnal eyes, but with spiritual eyes you can see
the fullness of the earth.

Reflections

DATE

Reflections

DATE

....

....

....

....

....

....

....

....

....

....

....

....

....

....

....

....

Luke 12:27-29

Consider the lilies, how they grow: they neither toil
nor spin; and yet I say to you, even Solomon in all
his glory was not arrayed like one of these. If then
God so clothes the grass, which today is in the field
and tomorrow is thrown into the oven, how much
more will He clothe you, O you of little faith?

A Nugget of Faith

During the Easter season, every year since my daughter became a
grown woman she has graced me with a lily. Jesus always comes to
mind when I see any kind of lily. The white Easter lily can be aligned
with Christ's humility, chastity, and purity from sin. The Easter lily
in particular gives off a sweet fragrance and is symbolic of the sweet
spirit of Christ that intermingles with your spirit. The words to the
hymn *He's Sweet I Know* comes to mind and speaks to the goodness
of the Lord to meet all of our needs. The chorus of the song says:
He's sweet I know,

> He's sweet I know,
> Dark clouds may rise,
> And strong winds may blow,
> Wherever I may go,
> That I have found a savior,
> And He's sweet I know.

It is His sweetness, His grace, and His mercy that allows us to spiritu-
ally flow through life knowing that all our needs will be met!

Reflections

_____
DATE

....

....

....

....

....

....

....

....

....

....

....

....

....

....

....

....

Reflections

_____

DATE

....

....

....

....

....

....

....

....

....

....

....

....

....

....

....

....

Ephesians 2:8-9

For by grace, you have been saved through faith,

and that not of yourselves; it is the gift from God,

Not of works, lest anyone should boast.

A Nugget of Faith

The Bible is repetitious and makes me know that God is always try-ing to tell us something. For example, the scripture above is basi-cally the same as Romans 3:24 and Romans 9:16. And, you will find that the previous scripture Luke 12:27-29 is basically, the same as Matthew 6:26-32. This kind of cross reference can be made in Matthew, Mark, Luke and John, as each gives an account of the life of Jesus. This kind of repetition makes me know God is trying to tell us something. I think God is always speaking to us. Unfortunately, many of us are not listening. Our ego, and our arrogance often pre-vents us from believing that anything is greater than ourselves. The truth is so simple that it is hard to believe that all. Further, we are so attached to ways of this world that we are hard pressed to change our mindsets.Commit to look inside yourself and the kingdom will be revealed to you. What the kingdom has to offer is so much greater than anything that the world has to offer. Make time to seek Him starting today. Meditate on the word, commit to it, believe it and receive the blessings of the Master.

Reflections

_____

DATE

....

....

....

....

....

....

....

....

....

....

....

....

....

....

Reflections

DATE

I Chronicles 4:10

And Jabez called on the God of Israel saying, "Oh
that You would bless me indeed, and enlarge my
territory, that Your hand would be with me, and that
You would keep me from evil, that I may not cause
pain!" So God granted him what he requested.

OH, THAT YOU WOULD BLESS
ME INDEED!

A Nugget of Faith

Bruce Wilkinson (author of The Prayer of Jabez: Breaking through
to the Blessed Life) refers to this scripture as a little prayer, giant
prize. Many people have used this prayer and referred it to others to
bring them peace in times of trouble, for protection in times of need,
to attract prosperity and to deliver them from evil. Personal experience with this scripture has brought deliverance in so many ways!
Try it for thirty days. Repeat it every morning upon rising and every
evening before retiring. Then count your many blessings!

Reflections

_____
DATE

....

....

....

....

....

....

....

....

....

....

....

....

....

....

....

....

....

....

....

....

....

....

Reflections

_____

DATE

....

....

....

....

....

....

....

....

....

....

....

....

....

....

....

....

....

....

....

....

....

....

II Corinthians 4:18

While we do not look at the things which are seen,
but at the things which are not seen. For the things
which are seen are temporary, but the things which
are not seen are eternal

Matthew 6:19-21

Do not lay up for yourselves treasures on earth,
where moth and rust destroy and where thieves
break in and steal; But lay up for yourselves
treasures in heaven, where neither moth nor rust
destroys and where thieves do not break in and
steal. For where your treasure is, there your heart
will be also.

READ and MEDITATE ON ALL OF MATTHEW 6:19- 25

A Nugget of Faith

A favorite guru of the modern day is Deepak Chopra. Chopra
gave us the Seven Spiritual Laws. One of the laws is The Law of
Detachment. In order to detach, you must fully understand that
everything in this world is temporal and will pass away. Detachment
is not wandering around aimlessly not caring about family, and trea-
sured memories. Detachment is about the full understanding that
this physical world (and everything in it) that you can see, touch, taste,
and smell will pass away. Therefore, it is important to be grounded in
SPIRIT and keep life simple! Do not be consumed by materialistic
things and all the white noise that occurs around you. Be still and go
with the flow of Spirit!

Reflections

_____

DATE

Reflections

DATE

....

....

....

....

....

....

....

....

....

....

....

....

....

....

....

....

GALATIANS 5:22-25

But the fruit of the Spirit is, Love, Joy, Peace,

Longsuffering, Kindness, Goodness.

Faithfulness, Gentleness, Self-Control

Against such there is no law.

And those who are Christ's have crucified the flesh

with its passions

and desires If we live in the Spirit, let us also walk in

the spirit

A NUGGET OF FAITH

Meditate on these *Words*. Whatever is unpleasing in God's sight ask Him to help you to walk in the fruits of the Spirit. Guilt can crucify you! Self-guilt can steal your joy and your peace. This is why you must learn to love yourself, forgive yourself quickly, and move on. You must also learn to be kind and compassionate towards yourself. Practice kindness, gentleness, and self-control over yourself by always treating yourself well. If you can learn do these things for yourself, it will be easy to do show the fruits of the spirit to others.

Reflections

_____

DATE

....

....

....

....

....

....

....

....

....

....

....

....

....

....

....

....

....

Reflections

_____

DATE

....

....

....

....

....

....

....

....

....

....

....

....

....

....

....

....

....

THE LORD'S PRAYER

MATTHEW 6:8-12

Therefore do not be like them.

For your Father knows the things you need

In this manner, therefore, pray:

Our Father in heaven, hallowed be Your name. (Line 1)

Your kingdom come. Your will be done on earth as it is in heaven. (Line 2 & 3)

Give us this day our daily bread. (Line 4)

And forgive us our debts, as we forgive our debtors. (Line 5)

And do not lead us into temptation, but deliver us from the
    evil one.

(Line 6)

For Yours is the kingdom and the power and the glory for-
    ever. Amen

(Line 7)

A NUGGET OF FAITH

This prayer is included in this book because I am amazed at how many people either don't know it; or they have not taken the time to dissect the profound meaning of the prayer. As I pray this prayer and dissect it, my soul seek to:

Line 1. Bless the holy name of God our Father,

Line 2 & 3Know that as above, so below, and my soul speaks to the multi-dimensions of the universe,

Line 4. Live in the now. Do not worry about what you eat, wear, or do tomorrow,

Line 5. Forgiveness is a key element, because who are we to ask for forgiveness from our father who is in heaven, if we cannot forgive our fellow man or woman,

Line 6. Let us not be tempted by the devil, who will attempt to tempt us daily,

Line 7.All power and all glory are with the Father!

**Learn the Prayer. Meditate on the prayer
and reflect on how The Lord's Prayer speaks
to your soul!**

Reflections

_____

DATE

Reflections

DATE

....

....

....

....

....

....

....

....

....

....

....

....

....

....

....

JOHN 3:5-8

Jesus answered, "Most assuredly, I say to you, unless
one is born of water and the Spirit, he cannot enter
the kingdom of God.
"That which is born of the flesh is flesh, and that
which is born of the Spirit is spirit." "Do not marvel
that I said to you, 'You must be born again.'
The wind blows where it wishes, and you hear
the sound of it, but cannot tell where it comes
from and where it goes. So is everyone who is
born of the Spirit."

A NUGGET OF FAITH

Water is one of the earth's five elements. Water, like all the other elements is vital to our existence. In fact, the human body, just like the earth, is made up mostly of water. In many ways water is symbolic. Baptism by water, and also the embryonic fluid that the fetus lives in for nine months is symbolic of the presences of the Holy Spirit throughout our lives. Spirit flows when the Holy Spirit is set upon you. You become a man (or woman) on fire when you preach the Living Word of God! Water is symbolic of the flow of Spirit offering life to us all. Learn to live in the Spirit and immerse yourself in the flow of the living water!

Reflections

_____

DATE

....

....

....

....

....

....

....

....

....

....

....

....

....

....

....

....

Reflections

_____

DATE

PEACE BE STILL

MARK 4: 35-41

On the same day, when evening had come, He said to them, "Let us cross over to the side."
other side." Now when they had left the multitude, they took Him along in the boat as He was.
And little boats were also with Him.
And a great windstorm arose, and the waves beat into the boat, so that it was already Filling.
But He was in the stern, asleep on a pillow. And they awoke Him and said to Him,
"Teacher do You not care that we are perishing?
The He arose and rebuked the wind, and said to the sea, "Peace, be still!" And the wind ceased and there was a great calm.
But He said to them, "Why are you so fearful? How is it that you have no faith?"
And they feared exceedingly, and said to one another, "Who can this be, that even
the wind and the searthe wind and the sea obey Him?"

A NUGGET OF FAITH

When you feel burdened and you think there is no way around circumstances that may exist in your life, use the power of the Word and speak to the storm you are in. Put your faith and trust in Him and ask for a path to open for you. Remember that all things work together for the good of those who love the Him (Romans 8:28). Even the things you cannot see (faith) are working for your good. God's way and His Word are what will bring you peace, that is still, and surpasses all understanding. Stillness is where you will find Him.

Reflections

_____

DATE

....

....

....

....

....

....

....

....

....

....

....

....

....

Reflections

DATE

....

....

....

....

....

....

....

....

....

....

....

....

....

....

....

....